T0039356

THE Poetess
REIGNS

THE *Poetess* REIGNS

A COLLECTION OF POETIC ART

JACQUELINE RAY-PHILLIPS

authorHOUSE®

AuthorHouse™ LLC
1663 Liberty Drive
Bloomington, IN 47403
www.authorhouse.com
Phone: 1-800-839-8640

Published by AuthorHouse   01/08/2014

ISBN: 978-1-4918-1252-5 (sc)
ISBN: 978-1-4918-1251-8 (e)

Library of Congress Control Number: 2013916068

Any people depicted in stock imagery provided by Thinkstock are models, and such images are being used for illustrative purposes only.

Certain stock imagery © Thinkstock.

This book is printed on acid-free paper.

This book is dedicated to my dear Mother, Juanita Ray. My Mother is by far one of the most influential forces in my life. My Mother taught me to always do my best. She would say, "no matter what you choose to do in life, be the best at it." When I look at my Mother, I see an enormous amount of strength and courage. My Mother is truly a force to be reckoned with. She has a heart of gold and loves her family deeply.

My Mother is a fighter. A very classy lady, filled with honor and a great deal of pride. She speaks her mind and she shoots from the hip. Throughout my life, all I ever wanted was for my Mother to be proud of me. With the creation of The Poetess Reigns, I am blessed and honored to dedicate this book to you Mommy. I will NEVER leave your side, even beyond the end of time! I Love You.

In honor of my Father, Luther William Ray, I love you too, Daddy!
REST IN PEACE

Jacqueline~

SIMPLY JACKIE QUOTES…

"Breakthrough the Breakdown."

"Listen to what they tell you… Know what they show you by action… For action is the ultimate Truth."

"I shall continue to dig deeper into self, for that is where I shall find infallible wealth."

"Action and the impeccable word are the Truth in Life and Love."

"When you choose to get naked in your mind and accept yourself for who you are, you are then able to Master the Art of Truth and Love."

Contents

ACKNOWLEDGEMENTS

I give Glory, Honor, Praise and Worship to All Mighty GOD, The Holy Creator of the universe, heaven and earth. I thank you Father for your Son, Jesus Christ. I thank you for this gift, the gift to write. I thank you for the courage to look inside myself and be honest and authentic with the truth of the words which you filtered through me. I thank you Father for choosing me as a vessel. I pray this book will touch many hearts and souls and transform lives as you so graciously did for me. I thank you for your favor. I thank you for your mercy. I thank you for your LOVE. ALL HAIL TO THE KING!

I give very special thanks to my husband, William Miles Phillips, Jr. for his love, insight and support of The Poetess Reigns. William has influenced me in a multitude of ways with regard to the rationale and hard core realities of several of my pieces. Thank you to my first born daughter, Jontel Dominyque-Ray Phillips, my sunshine. Jontel has been my biggest cheerleader throughout every aspect of our lives together, no matter the circumstances, she always has my back. We ride or die! I have enjoyed watching you grow into a strong, intelligent, educated, beautiful woman of GOD, with a heart deep as the ocean blue. Thank you to my baby girl, Miko Aliyah Phillips, my sweet joy. I appreciate your direct, straight to the point reviews of my art. Miko has been my Number One fan on all of our endeavors together. It has been pure joy watching you grow into a strong, beautiful, independent, educated, driven young lady with a heart of gold. Both of you are destined for success! I truly love you all.

I express special heartfelt thanks to my sister, Lori Ray Fisher, for her tired less efforts and unadulterated support throughout this project. She has shown an enormous amount of inspiration, encouragement and LOVE. I would also like to recognize my brother in law, Eric Fisher for his understanding and devotion. I appreciate my nieces, Taylor

Nicole-Ray Fisher and Morgan Bryann Fisher for their dedication and hard work during the organizational phase of The Poetess Reigns. Auntie loves you both dearly.

Humble and honorable thanks to Anderson Brown, Jr. a.k.a. "Papa," Godfather to my daughters, for your lifetime of support, love and encouragement to me and our entire family. You truly have proven to be the most kind and giving person I have ever known. The way in which you sacrifice and lend yourself for your fellow man is beyond admirable. I respect you and honor you to the utmost. Thank you for loving us. I love you dearly.

I wish to thank my Pastor, The Rev. Dr. Sherman A. Gordon, Founder of Family of Faith Christian Center. Thank you for your spiritual support and candor throughout the creation and development of The Poetess Reigns. Your motivation and inspiration is limitless. Thank you for your encouragement and the opportunity for me to share my "voice" with your valued audience on "An Evening with Pastor G." I also appreciate you pushing me to look deeper within myself to discover a myriad of poetic style.

I would like to acknowledge my dear friend and lifelong associate, Adair Williams for taking the time to proofread many pieces of my work and for his amazing brain power and richly desired feedback. Thank you for believing in me and encouraging me to "give it all I got and keep rising to the top."

The Poetess Reigns

Ready!

I'm ready to present the gifts that I hold
Ready to tell the world my story to be told
I've seen a great deal and I'm ready to shine
Get out and get on with my daily grind
I know out there is a position for me
GOD is gonna place me where He wants me to be
I needed time away to get my spirit right
And to conquer self-confidence and keep my mind tight
I have lived many struggles that could have took me out
But I am here now, ready to launch, scream and shout
If they don't understand me, really, it's cool
But after all this work, you'll recognize I'm not a fool
I dug deep in my soul and shared from my abyss
Hold on, take control, you don't want to miss this
Living in my past is something I cannot do
All I want is to bring my truth to you
I pray you all enjoy the truth brought from my heart
I had to relinquish the past for this brand new start
It's a new season, it's a new day
Bringing this raw, real truth straight your way
Sit back, relax and enjoy the ride
Thank you so very much for sharing with me your time

Gots To Do It!

Got to do it
Need to do it
Have to do it
Want to do it
Going to do it
Will do it
Must do it
You should do it
But whatever you do
DON'T QUIT IT!

Illumination

He gave me this gift to illuminate the world
He gave this gift to me, a Ramah Word, to a home-girl
With so much pain and anguish going on everyday
He sent me to tell the world there is a better way
Devoting your life to Christ will not lead to decay
For it is written . . . HE is the Truth, the Life and the Way
The words filtered through me are for the world to share
To tell you there is a Savior so you don't have to be in despair
I could go on and on and on . . . about His mighty works
This message is being shared to keep someone's mind from going berserk
Listen to me, understand, that the fat meat is greasy
For I can tell you of a way that is safe, yet not always easy
The enemy tricked me and stole a great deal
But GOD gave it all back and I now walk with a brand new zeal
My life is transformed, clearer and plain
No longer am I suffocated by that dark ugly strain
I am here to testify and tell you that this is real
Just ask Judas what happened to him after his last meal
We are all GOD's creation, equal in frame
Bow down on your knees and praise His holy name
If He did it for me, He will do it for you
He is using me as a vessel to bring this truth to you
In Jesus' name, Amen

Glory Be~

Glory be to God
I give it All to you
Glory be to God
I humbly thank you
For your Love is Amazing
Shocking and true
I can never live without you, Lord
Or else my life would be dreary and blue
The transformation you have made in me
Is real and raw
Ready for the world to see
For your Word is law
When the world sees me
It shall see you too
I won't let you down, Lord
That is my humble Promise to you
I LOVE YOU LORD, THANK YOU!❤

Standing

On the mountain top
Looking towards GOD
Standing confident
Due to His staff and His rod
Waiting patiently
Revelation of excellence
Transcending on a new path
Expecting to see the difference
Hopes and dreams all have been heard
To turn back just an inch
Would be completely absurd
Change of scenery
Change of venue
Mental health restoration
Faith food on the menu
A new exploration
Understanding the inheritance
Letting go of past ills
To marvel in His excellence
When they see me
They shall see You too
For with your guidance so clear, Lord
Your sheep will know exactly what to do
Prayer, praise and worship
The simple keys of three
Humble yourselves before Him
For He is gently descending . . .
Bow down on your knees
GET READY!

For Now I See

I can see a brighter day, Lord
Coming forward and intended for me
I pray and ask you to graciously hear my request
Please Lord listen to my plea
To remove the decay
Which once was rotting in my body
We are all apart of God's great strong army
If one part of me suffers
Other members meet and agree
Your promises are plentiful, gracious and raw
Fellowship begins within oneself
Ambitious and ready to rule as Your law
Your Holy word inspires deep within my soul
Your loving paradise is my ultimate and desired goal
Speak to me Lord, show me what is in my heart
My life is dedicated to You Sweet Jesus
I humbly thank you for my new start
My life was full of pain, uncertainty and madness
Yet it took being tossed in the stormy rain
For me to understand and comprehend your loving kindness
You brought me through without a blemish or stain
So magical and real for nothing I have done was in vain
So I had to endure the strain
So that I could stand and explain
The manifestation of my growth
In your precious and Holy name
So be it~

New Season

It's a new season
It's a new day
A bright new horizon is forming
Moving forward
Customized in your own way
The comet
The clouds
The birds of the air
With Jesus on our side
There is never a reason to despair
Drive and ambition
Dreams coming true
The Holy Spirit is in your body
Softly, gently running through and through
Time to relax
Time to sigh
Time to kick back
Time to wonder and ponder . . . why?
Nothing is by chance
Everything happens for a reason
Yea . . . Just like I said
Thank You, Lord, for it's a new season . . .

Ask, Seek, Knock

If you turn around too long your life can come to a halt
You will be straight on stuck like a pillar of salt
The past is the past
Whatever happened there will not last
Don't let it shape your mind
And steal or distort the images of future time
All things that happen are necessary and for a reason
But GOD gives us strength to face a brand new season
Going against your soul is destructive like treason
Upset and all confused and panicked like a heathen
These are a few of his tricks in store to behold
Remember he will do anything to rob and steal your soul
Lies and deceit are in his bag of tricks
But when you know who you are, he must flee, and quick!
Don't be afraid and do not fret
There is nothing too big that GOD has not met
There is nothing impossible for GOD to do
Ask, seek, knock . . . HE's at the door just waiting for you

Sweet King

Sweet King Jesus
You have brought me so far
My love and life with you
Has made me feel like a bright twinkling star
A life so precious and so dear
My Sweet King Jesus how I need you near

Grateful

Gratefulness is flowing from my Heart
With God by my side
I shall never fall apart
His promises are real
Time tested and true
Surrender your hearts to Him
So he can be a work of art within you

Sick

Sick to my stomach
Want to die
Sick to my stomach
Hoping to understand why
Do I ask?
Is it disrespect?
Will He even answer me?
Or is it just not time yet?
Where is His voice?
Where did it go?
Is He running from me?
Please don't leave me alone
The road is rough
And my companions are few
All the things I dreaded
May be coming near to me too
Disappointment, reality and shattered dreams
Perhaps I was delusional
Just making fluff in between
Hoping to be on the front line
Back to the end I go
What He has in store for me
Some day I hope to know
My palms itch with anticipation for the mean green
Did He throw me into the ocean to watch and hear me scream?
This world is full of crap
Ugly and strange
Please don't forsake me now
I need you to remember my name
Help me!

Holy Trust

I trust in
Lean on and rely upon You
My Faith is so strong Lord
I know exactly what to do
I give it All to you
For you are in command
I ask for my miracle now Lord
For only You can understand
I open my heart
And surrender to you
I Love you so much Lord
I'm doing All I am supposed to do
When the world sees me
I pray they see you too
The enemy comes strong to break me
He will attack anyone
To ruin my relationship with you
For my Faith is strong
As I am prepared to fight
Lord, with you on my side
I am confident that everything
Is already Alright!
I embrace my Love for you
With All that I AM
Open his heart Lord
And help him to truly understand
You are Almighty
Nothing is impossible for you
I surrender my marriage Lord
Show up! Show out!
Do that magical thing
Only you can do

Just A Thought

I know it's been a while
It seems you've pulled away
So much on my mind
So much I want to say
When you're given a dear friend
You must believe and share
No matter how special
No matter how rare
I awoke from my sleep
At three AM
The enemy pulled an attack
Yep, it was him again
Told me I was gonna have a heart attack
The shingles and even death threats
I rebuked him in the name of Jesus
For my life has only just begun yet
I arose strong mind ready to fight
Preparation for this test today
With an iron clad belief
Everything is already alright
So I began to write
For it is what I do
The following words and phrases
Came to my mind
And the spirit is burning for me to share them with all of you:
Confirmation
Affirmation
Appreciation
Stand on His Word
Preach to ALL Know
Never give up!
Believe

Prophesy
The Gospel
Jesus Christ
The Father
The Son
The Holy Ghost
The Truth
The Life
The Way
Inspiration
Adoration
Trust
Love
Fearless
Strong
Strength
Power
Glory
Obedient
Evangelist
Angel
Miracle
LORD!

Friendships

Friendships come in many ways
Different styles on different days
Ice breakers, chillers, popcorn and twizzlers
Understanding new meaning
Excitement, suspense and thrillers
A gentlemen, A gentlemen
Wow . . . Oh Wow!
Dreams do come true
Even now
Things that I see
Only God knows my heart
I will stand and wait
Don't want my emotions to fall apart
I hope I know what I see
I hope it is for true, for me
For with all that old baggage
I am uncertain what to do
God is in control at every season
Whatever is meant
God will be the reason
Is it another test?
A test of my faith?
I'm not really sure
Yet excited about the wait
God knows my heart
He knows it well
For when I look into His eyes
I know he can tell

Law Of Attraction

The law of attraction
Visualize the game
Understand your heart and passion
For your prosperity you shall aim
Success is within
Time tested and true
Living a life of Victory
Is no longer a stranger to you
Words are mere symbols
What does it all mean?
When preparing to become a champion
Living aloud the desires of your wildest dreams
Human beings and symbols
The world is surround
Don't allow them to pump negative in your head
And get your spirit and soul down
We have got but one chance at this life
So push the pedal to the ground
For success and happiness is victory you shall be abound
Therefore, never give up on your hopes and your dreams
Remember what His Words says . . .
Ask and you shall receive
You have not because you ask not
That remains to be seen
Stand firm on His word
Be patient and just believe

Peace

I feel peace in my spirit
Peace in my soul
Peace in my heart
Peace that cannot be sold
Prayer, praise and worship
Day and night
I did not miss the mark
I made it through just right
I know my request
I know it was heard
Wait for the manifest
Just as I was told
So many gifts
So many prayers answered
The devil is a LIAR!
My prophecy states there is no cancer
I walk by faith
Not by sight
Thanks to this trial
I know I did it right
Praise and worship
Scream and shout
He has lost again
For Jesus won the bout
Victory is ours
From beginning to end
Hold on to that outcome
When the trials begin
Always know there's a place for you to go
And His name is Jesus
For it is the sweetest name I know!

Humility

Patience and humility go hand in hand
Patience and humility, kick back relax and just stand
Stand on His word, His promises and virtues
Allowing my life to flourish like the ocean deep and blue
Emotions can run high, thick, murky and deep
For Your promises are the truth, which I know you will keep
Impeccability with your Word if only life could be the same
I Thank GOD for you Jesus and Your precious Holy name
Perhaps the path may seem bleak, desolate and dark
For if we place our Faith in You, we shall be confident to remain on the
mark
We must move by faith and not by sight
Lord Your word is alive, I must remind myself of that right
Proverbs, Psalms, Hebrews and Corinthians
Matthew, Mark and the Book of Thessalonians
With so much more Lord, I have only named just a mere few
Thank you for prophesy, Your word is the only thing that brings me
through
I search deep within my soul to find solace and peace
As your Word is my comforter, which keeps me humble and meek

The Circle

Maker of a circle
Maker of the twin
Measurement of a circumference
A sphere where the rains come in
Steady gentle flows
Given just enough
A place for you to go
When the outer world seems rough
The skies open wide
The clouds begin to form
A new way of living
Not quite the previous norm
A message so grand
Eloquent and exact
There is only one person who can deliver like that
Tear down the house
Is precisely what He did
Twirling in the circle
Getting everybody in
Round and round and round it goes
When to make it stop only He knows
Where all that energy resides is not unknown
Standing out doing that thing
Greatness is surely to be shown

Luther Ray

Luther Ray
Oh I hated when you went away
So early in life
Just didn't seem right
The love we shared
Has never been compared
Your love taught me how to feel deep and intently
I wish more people shared your special mentality
For so many years I didn't understand
With a Daddy like you, my life was just grand
Heart disease is what took you from me
For you are living with GOD now is what I tried to see
Your beautiful eyes and that cleft in your chin
I finally did it Daddy, now were going to win!
Oh my GOD how I wish you were still here
To sit down and talk to you in your favorite chair
I look forward to seeing you on the other side
I love you Luther Ray, until the end of all time

My Baby

Watch over my baby, Lord
Show her what to do
Watch over my baby, Lord
Let her express her Love for you
I don't pretend to know
The things that she has felt
By the decisions I have made
Perhaps made her scream for help
With you on our side we can endure
Our passion for you is strong
That is for damn sure
Watch over my baby, Lord
Hear my plea
Watch over my baby, Lord
For Jontel Dominyque-Ray still needs me~
I AM HERE BABY!
Simply Mommy❤~

Miko Aliyah

Miko Aliyah
My precious baby girl
Miko Aliyah
Your smile brightens up my world
Your drive and ambition
Never ceases to amaze me
You are strong and intense
Which only encourages me
Your future is bright
And blessed by the Holy Spirit
Your timing is always right
For you are a true scholar full of merit
My love for you is never ending
Miko Aliyah
You are so dear to me
Simply Mommy❤~

Sweet Sister

My dear sweet sister
How sweet the sound
My concern for you is genuine
Simple and ground
I can hear the struggle within
Each time that we speak
Even though you try and hide it from me
I pick up because I'm meek
Get your mind right Lori G
Don't allow it to get you down
At the end of the day
The perfect people will still be around
Dig deep within you
Not afraid to face the truth
You can't re-live the past
Nor the ills fated from both your youth
I see the distance deep in your eyes
But because you know me
I'm sure that's not a surprise
So, I will be here when you're ready to move
Look inside your soul
And never allow yourself to be fooled

Decay

The fear of decay
Watching her life slip away
The anger inside
Never seems to subside
What a day . . .
Watching my Mother decay . . .

Simply Lori Ray

Lori Ray
What can I say?
Lori Ray, you always make my day
The sweetest sister in the world is what you are
You have brightened my darkest days
Like the glowing evening star
We've traveled the roads hand in hand
When I was weak, there you stand
My love for you runs deep
Deeper than the abyss
So I use simple words like this:
I LOVE you Sissy!
We've been down in the trenches
Dancing on the pits of hell
But when I'm rolling with my Sister
I already know all will work out swell
You have seen my pain and my strength
My rock and breath
Because of you in my world
Even when I'm down
I feel your loving wealth
I could go on and on until the break of dawn
So I have to stop somewhere
For my love for you is no pawn
I LOVE YOU, LORI RAY
With ALL that I AM

Nieces

My nieces
Sweet nieces
How I love you both
When I think of my love for you
It puts a knot in my throat
Watching you grow
Loving you so
Letting you go
Only GOD knows
Auntie! Auntie!
Is what you say
Hearing that moniker
Makes my day
GOD is great
GOD is good
Seeing your adorable faces
Life is understood
Know that I Love you
Never doubt
If ever you need me
Give me a shout!
Nieces, sweet nieces
I shall always be there
No need to fret
Never be in despair

Steel Bottom

MEMO... Memo...
Where do I start?
The one and only who had controlled my heart
We met when we were kids
Babies at best
We've spent over a quarter century together
Our marriage, our lives had been a mighty quest
Your drive and ambition is raw and vicious
It would take an army of men to stop you on a mission
Everything you want always comes to past
Even the love, together we struggled to make it last
Gemini and Sagittarius, our signs connect
No matter how hard we fought, we tried not to lose respect
Our lives have been like a rocky rollercoaster
I stuck by your side, like your heat in a holster
That dimple on your cheek brightened their world
Even when you tried to give me away
I did not stop being your number one girl
A down ass chick is what I was for you
I have no regrets with us because I did what I had to do
Like a roller pigeon your life is complex
The way you tackle life
Not knowing what is coming next
An interesting man you have grown to be
Just a few things which mystified me

Everyday

Every day is not a perfect day
With the uncertainly inside of me
I want to scream in my mind and run away
Blow after blow
My body and spirit hits the flow
Hit after hit
Makes me wanna quit
But I must stand and deliver
Never to let my body quiver
PTSD
Yep, that's what they tell me
When that crap hits
My brain scatters like kibbles & bits
The pain is real
I don't even want to deal
Even if I run away
That ugly reality is here today
Today is all I have
Lightning strikes
And attacks the core like a bucket of crabs
I didn't understand
I thought I was ready
My hands shook like a windy tree
My grasp was not at all steady
That mood shock me really bad
Not appreciating the feelings of being sad
So I cope and rationalize
Allowing my mind to run and fantasize
Complexities woven deeper and deeper
Help me Father, you are my keeper
So I keep pressing, pushing on the grind
Simply stated, it's not even worth my time

Patiently

Several years of marriage
And I always have to fight
Earnestly praying to The Lord
Hoping we could get it right
Over twenty years of investment
With intense heartache and pain
Still wondering why in the world
I chose to carry that strain
Lots and lots of mistakes
Yes we tried to maintain
But something just ain't right
When you go against your grain
Seed time and harvest
I patiently wait to see
What GOD has in store . . .
Is there something better for me?
Obedience to His word is everything I want to do
Even if it meant being stagnate there too
Stepping out on Faith and waiting patiently
Seed time and harvest . . . GOD will deliver me
Miracles happen every day that I can see
By touching just the hem of His garment
I'm confident there is one in the storehouse just for me
So I continue to pray and wait oh so patiently
Thank you Lord, I'm tired, I shall wait and see
While I promise to give you praise and worship oh so respectfully
I'm calling out to you, Lord . . . I'm waiting . . . Come . . . Rescue me!

Pop Em!

Pop those pills . . .
Shit I don't care
Pop that pill . . .
Whenever my life is in despair
So much to deal with
So much to ascertain
I might try anything to erase the pain
Self-medication . . .
That's what's up
Feels like dedication
When I want to give up
Crawl in a hole
Pretend I don't care
Feeling all paranoid
People watching me everywhere
Will this feeling ever go away?
Dealing with this day after day
Why does it keep happening?
What's wrong with me?
I made changes in my life
Just has not snapped for me
I try and try to make sense of this world
Then I end up in my fetal position
All balled up like a baby girl
Pray for me!

For Life

Tucked away in a tiny cell
Tucked away in a place compared to hell
The dark, desolate and distant truth
Been locked away since they were a youth
With 10,000 days served on that bid
Life sentences passing away while the bodies are being hid
A concrete slave ship is what it should be called
While walking on the yard can easily get you mauled
So many of my brothers have taken this wrap
Running the streets in the 80's
They never knew it was the Nigga trap
Looking in the stainless steel mirror
Watching oneself age
Wondering, when in the hell will I get out this cage
It's takes a super human mind to roll and not break
But how much more are these individuals supposed to take
CDC blues is all they get to wear
Looking for a visit and nobody is there
Most of these people just need someone to care
Walking away from that visiting room
Your heart out it will tear
Vending machines, playing games, even lite banter
Yes, oh my goodness, these simple things all do matter
Time and dedication, you know how we role
Never again shall you feel you are the forgotten soul
One~

Perhaps

A charity case
Is that what they see?
A charity case
Is what they believe me to be
Handouts here
Handouts there
I make them uncomfortable
For in my face they cannot stare
Those same toxic feelings come rushing back
While I believe it's my character they want to attack
So what . . . I did not follow their norm
For it was I, the one thrown into the storm
Still loyal and down as I could possibly be
Perhaps if I had some support
Too, special I could be
The choices I made would have been different
Needing my mother's love
Synonymous with a newborn infant
Constantly being told you won't make it very far
Those words burned into my soul
Deep like the melodies of a string less guitar
Deep rooted dysfunction is all that I knew
Pushed me to the streets where different roots grew
I still feel inferior even at this age
Oh how I wish she understood the damage and my rage
Those deep inner feelings creep to my skin
I keep reminding myself
To allow the healing to begin
So I do what is fair
I always do my best
Dear Sweet Jesus
Allow me to put these feelings to rest

Unexpectedly

Now I have to do exactly what's best for me
Living my life complete and unexpectedly
Sacrifice of self was all that I knew
Even to the point where I am down and blue
No matter what the task I give it all I've got
While others roam the earth pretending like it's not
Not enough people in the world like me
Who will sacrifice themselves to make others happy
Betrayal begins at home from people of your start
They try and slip it in like its coming from their heart
Just keep living, eventually times will change
Playing with people's emotions is always a dirty game
Jealousy and envy all stems from pride
Gone on. I'm cool. I can't take that ride
Just never know what The Lord has in store for me
I will keep on living my life completely and unexpectedly

Laser Burn

Words can burn through your soul like a laser
The pain felt within cuts deep like a razor
Being careless with words can shock the body like a jolt
While the mind is racing
Running desperately like a baby colt
Images that can last for years to come
Eventually you must take a stand
Declare that's it . . . I'm done!
Sacrificing self for those who are in need
While they still pull at your life angry with greed
Understanding self-worth is a hidden treasure
When knowledge sets in that strain has no more measure
Proving yourself time and time again
No matter what you do you never seem to win
The ills of the past can haunt and cause you to choke
I just want to have peace and laugh at a few jokes
Be careful of what you say . . . Don't just try to win
Just think of yourself . . . How would you feel deep within?
Be mindful . . .

Trapped

Trapped against the wall
Banging my head
Doing my very best
Trying to remember what He said
Out in the ocean
Left alone
No one beside me
Seems like my strength is gone
It's a horrifying feeling
I must attest
Not wanting to face the world
The desire to retreat and get out of the mess
What did I do?
Where did I go wrong?
How could I have missed the mark?
We've been in the relationship so long
How long do I take to re-group myself?
Playing my best with the hand I was dealt
It's been a cool minute since I felt so bad
Tears gushing down my face
Angry, disappointed and even mad!
Mad at myself
For who do I trust?
Was it me?
Was it him?
Searching for clarity is a must
It's not about the gig
It's about my gift
I don't ever want to mistake His voice
For this I graciously admit
He is still with me
Forsaken I have been not
Gotta keep on pushing
If I don't everything I've accomplished will be forgot

Searching

Still great is your mercy towards me
When I awake and anxiousness is all I see
I feel the trembles taking over my nerves
Trying to determine why it's this I deserve
Facing a world that can be ugly and gloom
The devil trying to steal my mind and fill me with doom
Self-control feeling far away
Crawling out of bed trying to face another day
The pain in my back tight and gripping
Trying to understand and not get to tripping
So I do what I know best to do
Run to the medicine cabinet and pop a pill or two
I fight not to be led astray
Yet I must cope and get through this day
Tomorrow is always a new
I'm already looking forward to it
For today I do what I have to do
Yep, I got to do it
Discomfort and disdain
Makes it seem I'm going insane
There has got to be a better way
I will keep searching and looking for that brighter day

Everlast

Popping a pill
Trying to understand the pain
Back to square one
Did I lose or did I gain?
False evidence appearing real
God said He would not leave
He made me a deal
So I take my ticket to cash it in
To find there are others in line
Waiting to get a piece of the same meal
Why did it hurt me?
Why all the pain?
For we are women
Why do we have double the strain?
To go through labor
And to bear children in pain
A legacy of the curse
For all our energy it does drain
Then we have to work
And sweat from our brow
Gotta get my hustle on like a dude
Ain't no good if I give up now
So I wait and wait for more blows to come
I'm gonna punch on my Everlast bag
Until my victory has manifested and been won
So I reflect on past success
For I'm still a winner
Because I fall short of His grace
He still Loves me because I was born a sinner

To Roost

The pains in my stomach turn and burn
The knots and the turmoil causes my anxieties to yearn
Something taking my breath
As I suffocate and choke
Living life all carefree as if everything is a joke
My left side tingles with sensations like greed
I've got to get these toxins out of my body
For that is my greatest fulfillment of this need
Popping a pill hoping it will all go away
Unless I face my problems
This pain will be here to stay
Our bodies speak to us very loud and clear
The problem is most of the time it's saying something we not trying to hear
The true feelings of the core will always manifest
Get rid of that negative energy and allow your soul to rest
The spirit can get low and sometimes need a boost
As my Daddy would tell us:
"The chickens always come home to roost"

The Mirror

Looking in the mirror
I finally see me
A reflection that once intimated and petrified me
Looking in the mirror
I can see deep in my soul
A reflection so clear and real like the opening of a rose
A perfect breath of life waiting to unfold
Living a way of life that's better than silver and gold
The mirror reflects the image that we plainly see
Now I understand why the devil wanted to deceive me
The greatest gift we have is the gift of self
Once accomplished and understood we can attain the goal of GOD's
wealth
Living your life the way you are supposed to be
Is a gift and a goal to be reached perfectly
Never cheat yourself of the creation within
Being naked and raw with yourself is when life truly begins

Creeping

Often times we think the worst
The world can seem like a big ugly curse
Waiting for the world to shape and form
While symbols and customs drag us to conform
Seeing what is in our face looking for some kind of magic
When all that is clear is craziness and havoc
I know I am to be patient and believe
While everything inside me wants to burst and receive
Negative energy flows deep and strong
So tired of this crap
Where in the world did I go wrong?
I won't turn my back
I can't leave her all alone
Even when driven crazy and I'm left to my own
I fall to my knees and prep for the big fight
Desperately waiting for GOD to make everything alright
A lifetime of choices
Some special and some rare
When looking back on the mistakes
I know I was caught in the snare
Believing the un-truth
The distortions can be cruel
While trying to obey and not break the rules
No matter of their perception
I know what's in my heart
My real authentic self
Creeping back from my beginning
Back from my start

Certainly

Certainly it was He
That burst into my heart
And magnified me
Yes, for certain
It was He

Miles

He can be
A million
Miles away
But in my heart
He is here
To Stay

Questions Of The Quest

He makes me full fill a quest
Deep within myself
New ideas and thoughts
Back when I thought I could be bought
His courage I can see
Yet, how does that relate to me?
Inspiration to say the least
Hesitation can be a beast
I feel fresh and new
Even though I can be blue
No matter how I fight
These emotions are genuinely bright
So, I will not run
And I will not fret
I will be honest with myself
So that I will not forget
These gut feelings in my core are real
If I don't run away, how will I deal?
Opening up was simple and plain
So if I'm wrong for what I feel
Exactly who is to blame?
Complexities of life are not new to me
So I am authentic with myself
Enough to be whom I'm meant to be
The wind is blowing through my brain
With this type of euphoria there is never any strain
I struggle and struggle with all of my might
Sit, run, fight or flight?
Could it be conjunct?
Or thoughts and energies running off of luck?
Authenticity. Reality. True to character.
THAT'S ME!

Your Lane

Stay in your lane
Stop moving so fast
Learn to be patient
From the mistakes of your past
Perfect perfection resides within
We too are creators
For in our thoughts is where it all begins
Speak over it now
Encourage yourself
Pat your own self on the back
No need to wait for someone else
To KNOW who you are is a very special gift
Endurance of the tribulations
For our own good is never swift
Trust in, cling to, rely on The Lord
Keeping your spirit filled
Truly, you shall never get bored
Peeling back layers raw like an onion
I'm not going to be trapped again
Tucked away in that sick twisted dungeon
However it goes victory is for you
Stay in your lane
To thy own self be true

Sharing

Sharing of self is a precious gift
Living my life so fast
It was going by so swift
Twists and turns not knowing what to expect
Always keeping an open mind of what is coming next
Surprises and treats is what it all means
When he looks at me that way
He makes my spirit gleam
Energy and emotions run high esteem
Wondering what in the world does this one mean
Nothing is by chance I firmly believe
Happiness and peace is what I aim to achieve
Just when I thought I was out
He brought me back in
Now I need to roll with this and get back right again
Another new journey waiting to be seen
I wait with anticipation to find where it all leads
I discount nothing not like in the past
A brand new creation that could last and last
Taking nothing for granted is my new intent
Rolling with the punches if that is what's meant
Speaking my mind at each and every turn
Allowing the truth to effectively unfurl
So that nothing goes by plain and in suspense
Anticipating goodness at my very own expense
A new awareness, way of life, state of being
A new way of sharing the world, not just existing, but seeing

I Have

I've been through so much
I've worked so hard
I've prayed so long
I've lived through pain
I've given my all
I've fought many battles
I've casted out demons in the name of Jesus
I've fought giants
I've overcome adversity
I've stood
I've cried
I've overcome mental illness
I've battled depression
I've battled anxiety
I've battled addiction
I've battled infidelity
I've battled lies
I've battled the truth
I've battled court cases
I've battled disease
I've battled sickness in my body
I've battled unemployment
I've battled disability
I've battled criminality
I've battled my reality
Just a few things I've chosen to share
So you can understand the Faith which I declare
For without GOD I am nothing
For because of GOD, I AM everything!

Do What You Have To Do

Do what you HAVE to do
Do what you feel
Do what you NEED to do
For your life is surreal
Only you know you
And there is but I in me
Do what you have to do
To set your spirit free
Being pure with oneself
Is the ultimate gift and key
Sometimes it may get rough
And the path seems a little rickety
For that is it to trust
Which makes things best within us
Your system is full of small tiny cells
Growing and flowing
Like water runs into wells
The more you give
The more you get
The more you lie to yourself
The more to regret
I'm not certain about you
But I'm gonna do what I have to do

The Epicenter

Jesus is the epicenter of my life
Now that my world is committed to Him
I'm confident I will get it right
From turmoil and pain
And standing in the stormy rain
I now see that my life
Is beautiful, sunny and bright
From headaches and panic
A life that was completely manic
To Love, prosperity and gain
Now, I ask you
Can you stand the rain?

My Father

Thank you Lord Jesus
Thank you for this art
Thank you Lord Jesus
How I needed this brand new start
All of the times I have cried out to you
To bring me a life happy and brand new
I prayed and asked for you to hear my heart
I understand I had to wait to appreciate my part
For you are in me and I live for you
The longer the suffering
The greater my endurance grew
Forty-five years in the wilderness
Seems so very long
Yet now I can rejoice
And sing a brand new song
I know you are here Lord
And you won't ever forsake me
That gives me so much solace
Happiness, peace and glee
Your grace is amazing, Father
You saved a wretch like me
Now it's my time to be a prophet to the world
For within me, it is You they shall see

New Creation

A creation of self
The creation of life
The newness of me
Life without strife
The open naked truth
Dig deep within
Being real with ourselves
The healing can begin
Peace in my home
Peace in my skin
Living my life honestly
I'm excited and want to win
A long time coming
Waiting patiently
For at first I was blind
But now I can see

I Didn't Know

I didn't know I had a talent
I didn't know I had a gift
The enemy had stolen so much from me
My mind was left in suspense
The Holy Creator has shown me, me
For in the name of Jesus
I can be whatever I want to be
The trickery of the enemy
Man! He fooled me
But now I have been unleashed
Wait until they get a load of me
My spirit is humble
Precious and pure
I knew I had to be worth something
That's for certain and for sure
This flow, this gift
What a precious state to be
This flow, this gift
Has illuminated the Holy Spirit within me
God is great
God is pure
The truth, The life and the Way
He is ours, for the world, for sure
Surrender your hearts
It will not be in vain
For He is all knowing
And so very much worth the endurance of all the pain

Being Me

I am finally me
What an awesome place to be
By the grace of GOD
I can finally see
The true art
Of being me!

Time

Not to feel sorry for me
Time to feel power with me
So much change
So much new
In a pressed situation
Knowing exactly what to do
Definition of friends
Agreements to be agreed
Watching my prayers manifest
Is a distinguished event indeed!
Such an amazing experience
Which most certainly needs to be professed
I know the time is right
I know He has become
Gifts so grand and special
For only with God can this transformation be done
The days I cried
The nights I prayed
The stripping of my mind
For He never has been delayed
Trials and testimonies are a part of the game
In the event they happen
No need to hide in shame
This is a gift
This is a passion
The message must be spoken
The courage is prevailing
To get out there because its open
He gave me His Word
For me to share

A powerful team like God's
The enemy must retreat in despair
The power is strong
The power is intense
Unleash His truth
To no longer exist in suspense
It's Time . . .

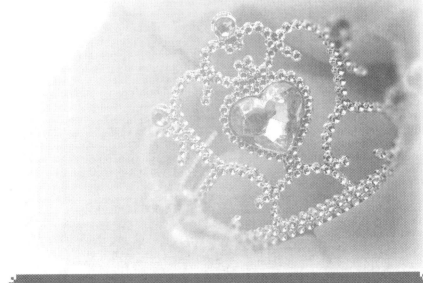

Free Of Toxicity

Trapped in a corner
Not able to breathe
Negative energy sucking at my life
Full of ugliness and toxicity
The pain in my chest
The pressure and the fear
Became overwhelming and vicious
Murder seemed necessary
And more and more clear
Gotta get my mind right
Self-audit and self-check
Balances of misery
Seemed like a noose around my neck
Hanging in suspense
Feeling like nowhere to turn
I had to get out of there
And let that piece of shit burn
Taking me for granted
Was so unkind to me
I casted my pearls before swine
For now I am free
To live a life that is finally mine
Becoming and befitting for a queen like me
Yep, that was me, living in the ugly world of toxicity . . .
Hallelujah, LORD . . . For now I am free

Listen

Listen to your body
Listen to the pain
Listen to your body
For it is not in vain
Ignorance is poor
Selfish and cruel
Your body speaks loud and clear
Listen and act for it needs knowledge for the fuel
Everything is connected eager to take the stage
When deprived of its needs
It will turn on you in a rage
Listen to your body
Simple and plain
Lister to your body
It is the source of your domain

Impeccable Word

Impeccable word
Now I see
Impeccable word
Reality
It did not happen
With me
Impeccable word

Forty-Two Too

When to let go
Now you know
When to let go
It was all a big show
Hopes and dreams
The lies he told me
Plans and schemes
He wanted to control me
Benefit of the doubt
That's what I gave
He wanted to get a hold of me
And make me his slave
Age is but a number
We all know that's true
While putting us asunder
Is what he really wanted to do
Actions and words
What do they mean?
Apparently nothing to some people
For I wait for what is to be seen
On and on and on he went
But at the end of the day
His word was bent
Poof . . . Be gone!

Waiting

Waiting in the dark
Waiting in the midst
Waiting seems so long
Like desperate travels to the abyss
The spirit is always willing
Yet the flesh is weak
I do my best to remain humble
To be gracious and meek
Turn the other cheek
Focus on something new
Continue the vigilant search
For out of it endurance will bloom
My faith is strong
Mustard seed to be exact
Lord, as I continue to pray
I can never be allowed to get off track
God will work it out
He will see you through
Don't worry your precious head
From Him, the creation will be brand new
Stress and anxiety will all go away
When first you trust God to bring a brighter day
Your calling is your calling
What are you to do?
Listen to your Heavenly Father
Be obedient and move
The struggles of the flesh can be constant it seems
For the Word of God is mighty
He promises to fulfill your every need
Receipt and acceptance of His gift to you
Is EVERYTHING He wants for you to do
Stand and WAIT…

Today

Today is a day of living the dream
Today is a day like never before seen
I'm walking by faith
Not by sight
Understanding my power
Letting go of the old fight
The masses are calm
Calamity put to rest
Standing on God's word
Putting the relationship to the test
Living by His promises
An experience which is new
Pushing my neurons to the limit
Fresh as the morning coffee brew
Expecting the goodness
Accepting His grace
Knowing His loving kindness
Makes us winners of the race
Gifts of silver
Gifts of gold
Gifts of the Promise
Never growing old
Open the self for questions
The magic of life begins
Maintaining the experience
Never again to be foreign

Seed Time & Harvest

Seed time and harvest
What about you?
Seed time and harvest
Angelic, prolific and brand new
A new way of life
Simple and free
A new way of life
Being what you were meant to be
Mindset, negative images
All in the past
The enemy wants to steal from you
Don't allow is trickery to last
We were born with a purpose
Steadfast and true
Everything you require to succeed
Already exists inside of you
So go get the shovel
Dig down deep within
Discover those gifts and talents
Never to be put away again

Feeling Blue

I feel a little lost right now
I feel a little blue
I feel a little lost right now
Not too certain what there is for me to do
Life is about choices
I understand that reality
But when I'm feeling down and blue
That concept seems more like insanity
My insides feel empty
Hollow like a waiting grave
I am doing my very best
To keep my head up and be brave
Uncertainty
Mystery
My life is filled with air
Now I need to get myself together
To hold on tight and to be aware
Life is a journey full of wilderness and trees
Gotta keep my mind right
Remain humble and drop to my knees

Me Too!

Shaking in my boots
Sweaty palms and hands
Shaking in my stilettos
Could this be my big chance?
Chances and destiny are put to the test
Freeing my mind from complexity
Allowing the natural abilities to attest
Reaping and harvesting
Planting seeds for growth
Looking deeper into self
Developing an extension cord on the rope
The Greatest . . . The Greatest, is what I want to be
The Greatest . . . The Greatest, is that not already me?
Stepping out on faith
The ability to believe
Standing firm on that faith
Is when victory is achieved
Tests, testimonies and miracles are true
Remember to stay planted
Whatever you're going through
His promises are real
Over 7,000 they include
We are heirs of Abraham's inheritance
Yes . . . ME TOO!

Spirit Free

Ride the ride
Ride the wave
Intensity enormous
Cannot explain
Absence of necessity
Release from constraints
Shake of the mire
No more complaints
Unleashed by the Creator
Break every chain
Strength and stamina
Like the stallion's domain
Breath of essence
Energy of life
Peace and contentment
Harmonious and tight
Liberation and independence
Power restored
Bondage and subjugation
Never anymore…

Fire

Playing with fire is a dangerous game
Maybe even a lowdown dirty shame
The heart racing
The body shaking
Searching for assistance
A humble existence
Chips are down
Who's there?
Like that . . .
Really?
Wow
Hanging in despair
Yes I can see
Was I ever blind?
Destructive hurt feelings
Ass out
Twisted in a bind
Tables do turn
Every dog has its day
Laugh now cry later
Until the Soirée . . .

BFH!

Some men will say anything to get in your pants
Like we supposed to be excited and do the happy dance
Stank filthy hands grabbing at your ass
Trying to get that thang without a cash advance
Man please! Come again! You must think I'm a fool
To kick back, chill out and wait on you
You got me twisted all up in the game boo
Go on and kick rocks or else I'm gonna have to clown you too!

The Wind

The earth is round
And makes rumbling sounds
The wind is free
Blowing away old debris
It whistles and blows
Around and up and down it goes
It's strong and it's wild
And oftentimes it could be mild
It carries an enormous amount of weight
Which I think makes it that much more great
It creates a soft summer breeze
On sunny days glistening through the trees
Picnics, sunshine and the ocean breeze
Grab that special someone and give them a strong squeeze
It can make you nippy
Maybe even cold
For until the end of time
It's might shall never get old
It pushes and pushes for the best from within
With this kind of energy on your side
You have encountered a very dear friend
A force, an agent that carries along an influence
Causing structure to stretch oneself
And to build higher for a greater prudence
A natural sophisticated movement of air
This style of talent is especially rare
Velocity speed and horizontal motion
Is so much more than just a mere notion
A simple breath
A simple speak
Allows the chimes of the wind to gather and meet
Percussion noise and general sounds
As for this entitlement
Ensures the earth's solid ground

Authentic

Authentic to self
The willingness of you
Authentic to yourself
Knowing what to do
Dreams and ambitions
Hopes unforeseen
Desires and cognitions
Blending tight and keen
Senses of one diving in the core
God opening the world
For so much more
Gifts and talents blossom within
With Jesus on our side
We are destined to win
Pick the self apart
Not afraid to be real
Specifications and customs
Are a dramatic aspect of the ordeal

The world turns
And so do we
Authentication of the personal
Is the key to being set free
Courage and strength
Are vital to success
Forgiving the past
Lost like a civil unrest
Bright futures
Colorful dreams
Positive energy
No low down dirty schemes
Feeling the power
Living your best
Anticipation and expectancy
Putting oneself to the test
AUTHENTIC

Moods Of Reality

Mood changes throughout the day
Pain healing and hurt can run astray
No matter what time of the day
We can always go to our Lord and pray
Blood pressure rises with anticipation
Oh my Lord . . . What is the explanation?
Turn fear into LOVE what a great gift
The mind has to be prepared
Logical and swift
The world is a melting pot
We all have basic human need
Step out of the comfort zone
And let go of the greed
Everything we need we have been equipped
I understand at times it gets hard
And you may feel whipped
Show us the way for the path is narrow
Will you give your fellowman a piece of your bone marrow?
Talk is cheap and action is key
For The Lord our GOD Loves us explicitly
A newness of life opportunity endless
Capture it and hold on
Be thankful for His forgiveness

Use Me

I have laid in my bed
Scared to death
Praying and hoping
I can't give up yet
Which way do I turn?
What to do?
Do I just stand in the rain?
Waiting desperately for you?
So I continue the fight
The good fight of faith
Hopes were up so high
I thought I had accomplished the wait
Then right back down
Deflated I felt
Why was I so crushed?
Why did my heart melt?
Trusting in GOD is what I'm supposed to do
Especially when I'm screaming inside
While it do what it do
The world is open
Time to get it in
Look closer and wiser
He gave you more than a lifelong friend
Use me . . .

Beyond The Look

The look is contact
The look is there
The look is magnifying
Subjects beware
The look is healthy
The look is strong
The look is dynamic
It can never be wrong
The look is fire
The look is wind
The look is a combination
Essence and purposes begin
The look is hot
The look is cold
The look is what it is
It should not be untold
The look is careful
The look is discreet
The look is meaningful
As the eyes lock and the corneas meet
The look is rich
The look is bold
The look is magical
It must never grow old
The look is mystery
The look is suspense
The look is discovery
Where friendships embark and commence
The look is this . . .

Asylum

Sickness in the brain
Emotions uncontained
Screams of despair
Blood splatter everywhere
Cries for help
Nobody cares
Where was the nurse?
Daily routine
Like a warden well aware
Gasping chokes
Catching your air
Games in the day room
Head cut with tears
Like a prisoner upset
In the distance stares
Structure serene
Like the snake pit
Lobotomy awaiting
Who really gives a shit?
Suffocation is freedom
Liberation from the nest
Asylum is the ultimate test

Daybreak

As I open my eyes was it danger I see?
Or a beautiful specimen lying next to me
He caressed my face soft like silk
We embraced in a kiss sweet as chocolate milk
He held my hand and stroked my hair
As I wondered
Is he really there?
My mind runs fast with pulsating body parts
If he comes any closer he will hear my heart
Beating strong pumping the blood
Fast with anticipation juices rushing like a flood
I want him to touch me
To touch me there
Should I tell him?
Oh no! I'm way too scared?
Yes! I have courage
I can do this
He has tinged my heart
I could only dream of a passion like this
An overmastering feeling convicted in my soul
Taking nothing for granted
His tender Love has broken the mold
I want it
I deserve it
I need to feel his strength
Delicate sensations yielding me against my sense

Climate Change

Temperatures change from time to time
Energy yours
Maybe mine
Kinetic stimulation
What a dream
Charisma and charm stuck in between
Gardens of Lillie's spring about
Walking along the shore in the midst of a shout
Skipping down the road headed to the unknown
Breaking through the chains
So much sweetness to be gained
Crashing sounds of the ocean blue
Sets off memories of the before you knew
Grit and grime between the toes called sand
Lovers embrace in a romantic stance
A simple kiss impressed upon my heart
Aggressive passion pierced like the point of a dart
Climate change

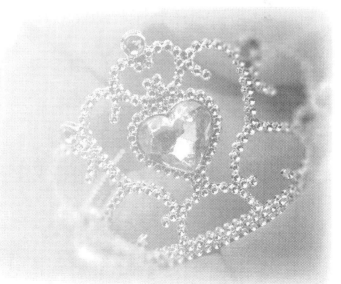

Beautiful spirit
Beautiful soul
Beautiful existence
Beautiful rose

Life experiences
Life renewed
Life so grand
Life brand new

Fire burns
Fire is flames
Fire acknowledges
Fire reigns

Wind blows
Wind is breeze
Wind whistles
Wind flows like trees

Ocean blue
Ocean sounds
Ocean waves
Ocean surrounds
The

Earth is round
Earth is divine
Earth is core
Earth is mine

Prophesy One

Our lives have already been bought and paid for by the blood covenant of Jesus Christ. Any and all things we go through, whether we deem good or bad is by our personal decision of perception. Jesus died on the cross so that each and every believer in Him, the Father and The Holy Spirit shall have everlasting LIFE. This means everything we will go through has already been signed, sealed and delivered into victory. The storm itself is a victory. There is a blessing in the storm. For the storm allows the ability for endurance and to exercise faith and commitment to the Word of GOD.

For in times of trouble, GOD wants us to have abounding faith and to stand on His Word and the promises He has offered as everlasting gifts to His children. There has to be a need for a miracle in order for GOD to produce a miracle so that we may marvel in His glory, goodness, kindness and tender mercies. It is often stated that perception is reality . . . Therefore, no matter the circumstances we are to be confident in knowing that all things work together for the good and that victory has been purchased through the blood covenant of Christ. The struggle can be the actual endurance of the flesh while going through the storm. The endurance of the punches and bruises and mental attacks while the fight is active. The ability to become and remain humble and patient during the trials and tribulations are the manifestation of our fleshly bodies proving that our faith is real and that our commitment to GOD's Word has been convicted within.

Please understand that every test and trial, hurt, heartache and pain is truly meant for our growth in Christ Jesus. We must understand and receive this during any test. Knowing your victory has already been won. Standing firm on His Word during the good and the bad. Whether happy or sad. We must praise GOD. We must pray earnestly. We must fast accordingly. For the enemy is real and he wants to catch you slipping so he can rob and steal everything you have. And everything The Lord, our GOD has in store for us. Stand on His Word. Be faithful. Be thankful. Be grateful. Be humble. Believe. Remain steadfast. And most essentially, LOVE. For LOVE is the greatest gift of all.

No Need To Fret

The past is dead and your future is bright. Do not worry about ANYTHING. Truly, I tell you GOD has already worked it out for you. You will know because your gut will tell you. Erase all the negative energy of your past. All the negative energy the world has caused. Today is a new day. You are a new creation in Christ Jesus. Trust and believe in your gut, your inner spirit. Because that is GOD, The Holy Spirit working within YOU. Take any feelings you may be unsure of to The Lord, our GOD. And He will give you undeniable clarity. At the right time and at the appropriate season. That is His promise to you. His Word is truth. Yesterday, today and forever more. You have an inheritance on your Life. By Faith, claim and receive your inheritance. Thank Him for it right now. And know that you are Love because GOD is LOVE. And GOD lives in YOU! If He did it for me, He will do it for you too!

The "Is" Factor

Nothing happens by chance
Everything Is
God Is
Truth Is
Love Is
Everything we need to survive
Is already within us
We were born to succeed in GOD's divine perfection
Then Satan and the world attacks
And fills our spirits and minds
With lies hate and deceit
But there is a Savior whom we can call upon
Jesus Christ, the Messiah, the Anointed One
He suffered and died for all of our sins
So that we could be made whole and live a life in Godly prosperity
He never said it would be easy
Yet, I am here to tell you that it is worth it
Anything you may be going through
GOD has already worked it out
Don't allow the enemy to steal anything else from you
For there is a blood covenant inheritance on your life
Keep praying fasting and believing
Never give up!
Because GOD IS!!

Prophesy Two

God grants us the desires of our hearts because He is the One who plants the seed of that desire within us so we may faithfully and earnestly pray, depend on and rely upon Him.

Understanding there is nothing too big for our God. As He is the Alpha and the Omega. The Beginning and the End. We as His children must become fixed and remain steadfast with the assurance that God is working things out for our good. There is no negative in Christ Jesus, therefore be on notice when those negative thoughts come, they are either coming from yourself and/or the enemy. That is the time to re-focus your thoughts on God. For He promises that if we keep our minds on Him, He will keep us in perfect peace.

Trials and tribulations are a part of the spiritual walk and relationship with God. Oftentimes, some new believers might think once they turn their life to Christ everything automatically is in splendor. I'm here to tell you that those trials are necessary so we may become stronger in our faith. Most importantly, so we may have a testimony to share with others who are new to the path. Knowledge is essential. No matter the circumstances, we must keep praying and keep believing in God and His promises. It would behoove us to live in a place of accepting and embracing the trials knowing that is the time for us to become closer with God, because we have His Word and His promises to stand on.

Go to Him. Talk to Him. Lean and rely on Him. God is not a liar. His Word is the truth, always. Yesterday, today and forever more. Praise Him. Worship Him. Love Him. Most of all TRUST Him. For He is waiting to open the flood gates of heaven upon us. In Jesus' name, Amen.

Thank You

Thank you for making me better
Thank you for making me whole
By faith in my spirit
My life to Christ
Dear GOD Behold
Being in so much pain
Anguish and doubt
It had been hard for me
To lift my hands and shout
But I know a Man
Who died on the cross
For sinners like myself
Sheep who were lost
Faith is a precious gift
Which grows from within
Patience and endurance
Is when it all begins
Fight the fight
The good fight of faith
Fast and pray with reverence
During the tedious wait
My GOD! My GOD!
You did not forsake me
My GOD! My GOD!
You continue to Bless me
O Sovereign GOD
Creator of my heart
Thank you for this gift
Thank you for my art